A Model of Servant Leadership

140 Bite-Sized Ideas to Build Your Heart for Servant Leadership

Mark W. Deterding

An Actionable Business Journal

E-mail: info@thinkaha.com
20660 Stevens Creek Blvd., Suite 210
Cupertino, CA 95014

Published by THiNKaha®
20660 Stevens Creek Blvd., Suite 210, Cupertino, CA 95014
http://thinkaha.com
E-mail: info@thinkaha.com

First Printing: March 2016
Paperback ISBN: 978-1-61699-178-4   1-61699-178-X
Hardcover ISBN: 978-1-61699-179-1   1-61699-179-8
eBook ISBN: 978-1-61699-180-7   1-61699-180-1
Place of Publication: Silicon Valley, California, USA
Paperback Library of Congress Number: 2016933251

Trademarks

Warning and Disclaimer

Dedication

To my wife, Kim, for her never-ending support and encouragement in my endeavors of building a business to spread the word on servant leadership to positively impact the world. She is a great model for me each day.

This book is also dedicated to:

- My children, David and Dan, and their families, who are just as passionate about servant leadership as I am.

- My Mom and Dad, who modeled this kind of servant leadership their entire lives but never used the term "servant leadership."

- My coaching clients, who inspire me every day with their heart and passion for servant leadership and their desire to change the world.

Acknowledgements

Special thanks to my wife, Kim, for putting up with my passion for this business and the time it has taken from our family.

Thanks to Jane Anderson for her amazing heart for servant leadership and how she relentlessly serves so many people within her life. She had a significant positive impact on this book with her writing and editing skills.

Thanks to Chris Edmonds, my culture coach and friend, who has taught me so much about the process of driving a purpose-driven, values-based culture and who encouraged me to write this book.

Thanks to the many past leaders that I had the opportunity to work for and learn from over the years, which led to the formation of the Triune Leadership Services Model of Servant Leadership.

Thanks to Mitchell Levy and the entire THiNKaha team for their efforts and enthusiastic support of the *A Model of Servant Leadership* addition to the THiNKaha series.

Why I Wrote This Book

- I want to advance my personal purpose of "Glorifying God by helping leaders to lead at a higher level, to enable them to achieve their God-given potential, and to make a significant positive impact on the world."
- I want to provide an easy and efficient way for leaders to build their heart for servant leadership.
- I want to share what I have learned from the many great leaders I have been blessed to work with, to shorten the learning curve of effective servant leadership.
- I want to build momentum for a movement of servant leadership across the country.

Mark Deterding

Founder/CEO of Triune Leadership Services, LLC

http://www.triuneleadershipservices.com/
https://twitter.com/mwdeterding
https://www.facebook.com/liveleadlove
https://www.linkedin.com/in/markdeterding

How to Read a THiNKaha® Book
A Note from the Publisher

The THiNKaha series is the CliffsNotes of the 21st century. The value of these books is that they are contextual in nature. Although the actual words won't change, their meaning will change every time you read one as your context will change. Experience your own "aha!" moments ("AhaMessages™") with a THiNKaha book; AhaMessages are looked at as "actionable" moments—think of a specific project you're working on, an event, a sales deal, a personal issue, etc. and see how the AhaMessages in this book can inspire your own AhaMessages, something that you can specifically act on. Here's how to read one of these books and have it work for you:

1. Read a THiNKaha book (these slim and handy books should only take about 15–20 minutes of your time!) and write down one to three actionable items you thought of while reading it. Each journal-style THiNKaha book is equipped with space for you to write down your notes and thoughts underneath each AhaMessage.

2. Mark your calendar to re-read this book again in 30 days.

3. Repeat step #1 and write down one to three more AhaMessages that grab you this time. I guarantee that they will be different than the first time. BTW: this is also a great time to reflect on the actions taken from the last set of AhaMessages you wrote down.

After reading a THiNKaha book, writing down your AhaMessages, re-reading it, and writing down more AhaMessages, you'll begin to see how these books contextually apply to you. THiNKaha books advocate for continuous, lifelong learning. They will help you transform your ahas into actionable items with tangible results until you no longer have to say "aha!" to these moments—they'll become part of your daily practice as you continue to grow and learn.

As the Chief Instigator of Ahas at THiNKaha, I definitely practice what I preach. I read *Alexisms* and *Ted Rubin on How to Look People in the Eye Digitally*, and one new book once a month and take away two to three different action items from each of them every time. Please e-mail me your ahas today!

Mitchell Levy
publisher@thinkaha.com

Contents

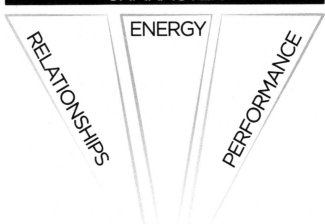

MODEL OF SERVANT LEADERSHIP

CHARACTER

ENERGY

RELATIONSHIPS

PERFORMANCE

FOUNDATION

Section I

Build the Foundation

Servant leadership starts by Building the Foundation. The AhaMessages that follow define the components of the foundation and its importance to the organization.

1

#ServantLeaders begin the journey by building the foundation, guided by a well-articulated purpose, vision, and values. @mwdeterding

_____

_____

_____

2

We don't live segmented lives. Purpose, vision & values are who we are at work, home, church & community. @mwdeterding

_____

_____

_____

3

Infusing your soul with your purpose, vision & values makes a firm foundation. Sharing them keeps you accountable.
@mwdeterding

_____

_____

_____

4

Deepen your resolve toward living a life of meaning as you live within your declared purpose, vision & values. @mwdeterding

_____

_____

_____

5

Commit to be molded by the Master. Let your vision and values be formed by Jesus. Philippians 2:5-6. @mwdeterding

_____

_____

_____

6

Do your teams internalize your
organization's purpose, vision & values?
Start now to build that foundation.
@mwdeterding

_____

_____

_____

7

Shared purpose and vision hold the power
to move your organization forward.
@mwdeterding

_____

_____

_____

8

When people align with organizational purpose & values, their sense of connection, belonging & loyalty is enhanced.
@mwdeterding

_____

_____

_____

9

Effective meetings are driven by purpose, values & priorities. If any of these are missing, rethink the meeting. @mwdeterding

_____

_____

_____

10

Even when challenged, stand firm on your purpose and values. Stand for something, or you will fall for anything. @mwdeterding

_____

_____

_____

11

Tap into your own purpose, talents & creativity to help inspire purpose, talents & creativity in others. @mwdeterding

_____

_____

_____

12

Build your organization on top of the foundation of a compelling purpose, knowing that everything else will follow. @mwdeterding

_____

_____

_____

13

A compelling purpose provides the impetus & passion for action. It answers the question: Why do we exist? @mwdeterding

_____

_____

_____

14

Key skills of #ServantLeader visionaries: Insightful, Creative, Curious, Courageous, Strategic, Receptive, Collaborative. @mwdeterding

_____

_____

_____

15

A clearly articulated vision establishes leadership and creates clarity, energy, focus, and accountability. @mwdeterding

_____

_____

_____

16

Vision is a picture of a preferred future that answers the question: What do we want to create? @mwdeterding

_____

_____

_____

17

Does your team share your vision? Is it so clear, they answer yes when you ask, "Can you see what I see?" @mwdeterding

_____

_____

_____

18

Describe your vision in vivid detail. If your vision is fuzzy to you, it will certainly be foggy to those you lead. @mwdeterding

_____

_____

_____

19

Where there is no vision, the people perish; blessed are they who heed wisdom & instruction. Proverbs 29:18 @mwdeterding

_____

_____

_____

20

Values are enduring beliefs you seek to
attain, which define the fundamental culture
of the organization. @mwdeterding

_____

_____

_____

21

Values answer the question: How are we going to behave? They define the culture of the organization. @mwdeterding

_____

_____

_____

22

#ServantLeaders cultivate values by discussing them and reinforcing them openly and often every day. @mwdeterding

_____

_____

_____

23

#ServantLeaders clearly define values by articulating specific behaviors that align w/ them, then daily model those behaviors. @mwdeterding

_____

_____

_____

24

Cultivate, protect & steward the Foundation of your organization. Purpose, Vision, Values, Strategy & Priorities. @mwdeterding

_____

_____

_____

Section II

Build Energy

Once the Foundation is set, servant leaders
Build Energy within the organization to most
effectively achieve the purpose and vision.
The AhaMessages in this section define
ways to Build Energy.

25

How is the energy level in your organization? Give it a boost! Recognize & encourage people for their great work. @mwdeterding

_____

_____

_____

26

Get out from behind your desk & walk the floor every day. Know the names of every person & their spouse's, too. @mwdeterding

_____

_____

_____

27

There are no coincidences in God's plan.
Who has He put in your path today to uplift
and encourage? @mwdeterding

_____

_____

_____

28

The most important gift you can give is your attention. Through it, you add value to others & make significant impacts. @mwdeterding

_____

_____

_____

29

When you speak into lives today, what words will you use to instill confidence & give hope, peace, comfort & joy? @mwdeterding

_____

_____

_____

30

Attitudes are contagious and influence others. What attitudes are people catching from you? @mwdeterding

_____

_____

_____

31

Taking care of yourself is not selfish. It is mandatory so you are at your best & able to effectively serve others. @mwdeterding

_____

_____

_____

32

In meetings, #ServantLeaders ensure that the team is working toward supporting the vision and advancing the purpose. @mwdeterding

_____

_____

_____

33

People need to feel like they belong, their work matters & they are contributing to the success of the organization. @mwdeterding

_____

_____

_____

34

To shape a culture, become a storyteller sharing memorable facts that inform, entertain, educate & inspire. @mwdeterding

_____

_____

_____

35

What can you do to impress on someone that their position, even if obscure, is irreplaceable to the organization? @mwdeterding

_____

_____

_____

36

Don't put off till tomorrow the good you can do today. Appreciate, value & encourage others with affirmations. @mwdeterding

_____

_____

_____

37

Taking a "Coach Approach" promotes
self-discovery in people & encourages
them toward mastery of their destinies.
@mwdeterding

_____

_____

_____

38

Set appropriate boundaries for people's
competency & passion, then allow them to
do their work, without pressure.
@mwdeterding

_____

_____

_____

39

#ServantLeaders understand the positive impact of allowing people to use their brains, not just their hands and feet. @mwdeterding

_____

_____

_____

40

#ServantLeaders encourage people to innovate, by accepting risk and learning from failures along the way. @mwdeterding

---

41

#ServantLeaders are encouragers, praising people for doing the right things. Be specific and sincere. @mwdeterding

---

42

#ServantLeaders greatly value providing positive recognition and making it a daily activity. @mwdeterding

_____

_____

_____

43

A kind word, a compliment, an expression
of gratitude, and saying "I believe in you"
are all life-giving words. @mwdeterding

_____

_____

_____

44

People are hungry for appreciation. Be the #ServantLeader who encourages innovation and recognizes genuine effort. @mwdeterding

_____

_____

_____

45

Start a trend: Recognize someone every day for doing the right thing or living out the values of the organization. @mwdeterding

_____

_____

_____

46

Celebrity is all about you. Celebrations are all about them. Celebrate achievements with your team, for your team.
@mwdeterding

_____

_____

_____

47

What is one thing you do every day to assure team members know they are valued & their contributions are appreciated?
@mwdeterding

_____

_____

_____

48

Does your attitude reflect gratitude? Filling your soul with thanks will lead to good health & positive outlook on life. @mwdeterding

_____

_____

_____

49

Do you spend or invest time in people?
Spend it & it's gone. Investing
in it multiplies. Be an investor;
take the long view. @mwdeterding

_____

_____

_____

50

Recognize the best investment you can
make is spending time with your team,
likewise with your children! @mwdeterding

_____

_____

_____

Section III

Build Performance

Servant leaders help people and
organizations achieve great things. The
AhaMessages in this section illustrate ways
to Build Performance within an individual,
family, team, or organization.

51

Challenge the status quo leading your team to develop a mindset of continuous improvement and premium service. @mwdeterding

_____

_____

_____

52

#ServantLeaders foster a culture of continuous improvement. Innovation isn't born from status quo thinking. @mwdeterding

_____

_____

_____

53

Be a lightning rod for high performance. Be passionate about personal discovery & development. @mwdeterding

_____

_____

_____

54

#ServantLeaders have a heart for learning & a passion for personal development. Position yourself to make that happen. @mwdeterding

_____

_____

_____

55

We become like those who influence us. Surround yourself with positive people who challenge you to grow. @mwdeterding

_____

_____

_____

56

Have a passion for personal development so you are continuously becoming the best for the people you are serving. @mwdeterding

_____

_____

_____

57

Recognize the best way to build performance is to hire and develop a "Dream Team." It won't happen without great people. @mwdeterding

_____

_____

_____

58

#ServantLeaders hire first for values, then for talent, then for experience. In that order. Don't shortcut the process. @mwdeterding

_____

_____

_____

59

#ServantLeaders assess their team by observing both values performance and technical / job competencies. @mwdeterding

_____

_____

_____

60

#ServantLeaders create clear expectations, monitor progress regularly, and coach and redirect as necessary. @mwdeterding

_____

_____

_____

61

Provide the gift of honest feedback out of love for others & recognition of their potential for development. @mwdeterding

_____

_____

_____

62

Develop a learning culture: Each one teaches one. "As iron sharpens iron, one sharpens another." Proverbs 27:17 @mwdeterding

_____

_____

_____

63

The highest performing athletes have numerous coaches. It is the same with high-performing #ServantLeaders.
@mwdeterding

_____

_____

_____

64

#ServantLeaders are not concerned about advancing themselves; instead, they focus on how far they can advance others.
@mwdeterding

_____

_____

_____

65

Take a "Coach Approach" to help people reach their potential. Encourage them to discover & channel their strengths. @mwdeterding

_____

_____

_____

66

People are not projects, they are souls
with potential. Help people discover their
strengths & find places to use them.
@mwdeterding

_____

_____

_____

67

To create a culture of growth & opportunity,
consistently recognize strengths & potential
in individuals. @mwdeterding

_____

_____

_____

68

Others-centered #ServantLeaders coach and support. Self-centered leaders coerce and dominate. @mwdeterding

_____

_____

_____

69

Coaching & mentoring adds value to people, lifts them up, and helps them advance & become who they were born to be. @mwdeterding

_____

_____

_____

70

#ServantLeaders ensure that everyone has annual improvement goals, which provide clear priorities for the year. @mwdeterding

_____

_____

_____

71

To help someone achieve their goals, you must get to know them. Help them find their why so they can find their way. @mwdeterding

_____

_____

_____

72

To make a difference, you have to be different. Be quick to instruct, correct & encourage through positive influence. @mwdeterding

_____

_____

_____

73

Punishment says: You'll never learn!
Coaching says: What can we learn from
this? Change language, change behavior.
@mwdeterding

_____

_____

_____

74

Bring people into accountability with you so they are continually improving themselves & modeling it for others. @mwdeterding

_____

_____

_____

75

Value of 1x1 meetings: shows respect, provides focus, supports ambitions, fosters relationship, and encourages feedback.
@mwdeterding

———————————————————————————

———————————————————————————

———————————————————————————

Section IV

Build Relationships

Servant leaders understand that anything
positive happens through relationships.
The AhaMessages in this section explain ways
to be intentional about Building Relationships.

76

Recognize the intrinsic value in people
& find ways to convince them of that fact.
Ready? What is your next step?
@mwdeterding

_____

_____

_____

77

Transparency is a catalyst for building
relationships: Willingly recognize,
understand, and honor differences.
@mwdeterding

_____

_____

_____

78

Look at people & see potential, not problems. What can you do today to encourage your masterpieces in the making? @mwdeterding

---

79

Personally acknowledging people is the "blocking & tackling" of building relationships. @mwdeterding

---

80

Relationships start with a conversation and a conversation starts with just one question. @mwdeterding

_____

_____

_____

81

Building relationships is not a spectator sport. Bring your best game to work, starting with your attitude. @mwdeterding

_____

_____

_____

82

"Let no one come to you without leaving better & happier. Be the living expression of God's kindness." -Mother Teresa @mwdeterding

_____

_____

_____

83

What gets you up in the morning? Get up to pour value into people by listening, caring, encouraging, and inspiring. @mwdeterding

_____

_____

_____

84

#ServantLeaders help others discover their why, let them experiment with the how, and open doors to their way. @mwdeterding

_____

_____

_____

85

What can you do today to make someone feel valued? Use life-giving words. Actively listen. Say thank you. @mwdeterding

_____

_____

_____

86

Do you want a high-performing organization? Create a culture of receptive, empathetic listeners. Listen, then respond. @mwdeterding

_____

_____

_____

87

Listen to understand, hear the unspoken word & ask thoughtful questions. Know people have great ideas & answers. @mwdeterding

_____

_____

_____

88

You cannot lead with an open heart if you have a closed mind. Be a good listener, free of distractions & without filters.
@mwdeterding

_____

_____

_____

89

Hearing & listening are different. To hear, use your ears. To listen, use your senses. To understand, use your heart. @mwdeterding

_____

_____

_____

90

Listen at heart level. Be present. Turn your attention so it's "in here" and not distracted by what's "out there." @mwdeterding

_____

_____

_____

91

Listen more, talk less, is not just cliché. Listening is the foundation of understanding and leadership. @mwdeterding

_____

_____

_____

92

To be a better leader, be a better listener. Effective listeners learn more and understand more. @mwdeterding

_____

_____

_____

93

Having a heart to serve and acting naturally out of love for others is the foundation of #ServantLeadership. @mwdeterding

_____

_____

_____

94

Mistakes are inevitable, forgiveness a choice. Learn from the past & move forward. Never let a setback become a stay back. @mwdeterding

_____

_____

_____

95

#ServantLeaders love life and they love people. This is why they can both lead and serve. @mwdeterding

_____

_____

_____

96

#ServantLeadership is about being full of joy, gratitude, and compassion for those you are serving. @mwdeterding

_____

_____

_____

97

Formula for valuing people and building relationships: Respect + Support + Listen + Understand + Love + Forgive + Trust. @mwdeterding

_____

_____

_____

Section V

Build Character

The entire model of servant leadership falls apart if you are not a person of high character. The AhaMessages in this section share ways to build trust and enhance your personal character.

98

#ServantLeaders are called to serve & be stewards of the organization's purpose, values & vision. @mwdeterding

_____

_____

_____

99

"No one knows less about humility than he who is truly humble." -Martin Luther. #ServantLeadership requires humility. @mwdeterding

_____

_____

_____

100

Trust takes a lifetime to build and 5 seconds to lose. What are you doing to build & maintain a foundation of trust? @mwdeterding

_____

_____

_____

101

To model integrity, start by praying for God to guard your heart and guide your mind in every decision. @mwdeterding

---

102

To be a leader others want to follow, be a person who has the qualities you would want to follow. @mwdeterding

---

103

Trust is not a task; it is a trait. Trust is not bought; it is earned by an intentional focus on your character. @mwdeterding

---

104

Lead with trust, show respect to everyone, be honorable, and you will gain people's trust. @mwdeterding

---

105

To live the same values that are posted on your wall is to live with integrity. Do what you say you will do. @mwdeterding

_____

_____

_____

106

Create a peaceful and productive work environment. Cultivate optimism & trust.
@mwdeterding

_____

_____

_____

107

#ServantLeadership measures success not in status and financial gain but in excellence of character and integrity. @mwdeterding

_____

_____

_____

108

Values are communicated through your actions & must authentically represent your foundation: purpose, vision, & values. @mwdeterding

_____

_____

_____

109

#ServantLeaders model & set the pace. Be one who transfers your vision to your teams, activating passion & energy. @mwdeterding

_____

_____

_____

110

Be intentional about adding value to others; live a life that is significant and impactful. @mwdeterding

_____

_____

_____

111

Keys that develop moral authority: Trust others. Have integrity. Set appropriate boundaries. Delegate to others. @mwdeterding

_____

_____

_____

112

"Humility is not thinking less of yourself,
it's thinking of yourself less." -C.S. Lewis.
Demonstrate a character of humility.
@mwdeterding

_____

_____

_____

113

Position, power, gender & stature are not prerequisites of #ServantLeadership. Trust is the key to leadership and influence. @mwdeterding

_____

_____

_____

114

When people trust you, they will follow without fear of where you are taking them. @mwdeterding

_____

_____

_____

115

#ServantLeaders build character by aligning their actions with their words on a consistent basis. @mwdeterding

_____

_____

_____

116

Seek godly wisdom, step out in faith, walk a courageous path, practice integrity, build trust & teach it to others. @mwdeterding

_____

_____

_____

117

Earn trust through honesty & vulnerability, being present & approachable & align your actions with your words. @mwdeterding

_____

_____

_____

118

Self-centered dominates. Others-centered supports. Think about it. What is at your center? #ServantLeadership @mwdeterding

_____

_____

_____

119

Leaders, you cannot get these at your command: Respect, Trust, Honor, Loyalty. They are earned. @mwdeterding

_____

_____

_____

120

Our roles in life are not separate from character. Character is who we are at work, home, church, or community. @mwdeterding

_____

_____

_____

121

There is no entitlement to trust. Trust is earned through consistent moral, ethical proof of character. @mwdeterding

_____

_____

_____

Section VI

The Secret

We have the opportunity to call upon a higher power to help us become effective servant leaders. The AhaMessages in this section reveal the secret to being a person of significance.

122

What if you started this week by saying, "God equip me for your service." How would your week be different? @mwdeterding

_____

_____

_____

123

Jesus is the ultimate model of
#ServantLeadership. He was intentional
about changing lives through compassion &
relationships. @mwdeterding

_____

_____

_____

124

Be a game changer. Make prayer your first
response, not your last resort.
@mwdeterding

_____

_____

_____

125

God is at the heart of #ServantLeadership. "Without God's help, I cannot succeed, but with it, I cannot fail." -Abraham Lincoln @mwdeterding

_____

_____

_____

126

A legacy of #ServantLeadership: Walk beside others, train, mentor, model & pray for people in your sphere of influence. @mwdeterding

_____

_____

_____

127

#ServantLeadership mindset based on 1 Corinthians 9:19 - I have made myself a servant to all, that I might win more of them. @mwdeterding

_____

_____

_____

128

"Truth is entrusted to faithful men so that they might teach others." -2Timothy 2:2 #ServantLeadership @mwdeterding

_____

_____

_____

129

God gave us talents & passions to advance His Kingdom. These gifts are woven into the tapestry of #ServantLeadership.
@mwdeterding

_____

_____

_____

130

Pour into others from a heart knowing "the one who has been entrusted with much, much more will be asked." -Luke 12:48
@mwdeterding

_____

_____

_____

131

Jesus is the ultimate model of #ServantLeadership. What is your modern-day equivalent of washing the feet of others? @mwdeterding

_____

_____

_____

132

Never doubt the power of God. Read His Word with an open heart. He has an answer for every challenge. @mwdeterding

_____

_____

_____

133

Take faith not fear to work. Faith encourages, hopes, connects & renews. Fear doubts, impedes, constrains & confuses. @mwdeterding

_____

_____

_____

134

God is calling you not to a life of self-service but to a life of selflessness & edification of others. 2 Thes 1:11 @mwdeterding

_____

_____

_____

135

#ServantLeadership: Live your life in such
a way that those who don't know God will
want to know Him because they know you.
@mwdeterding

_____

_____

_____

136

The more you remember about people (name, birthday, strengths, interests), the more they know you truly care about them. @mwdeterding

_____

_____

_____

137

The secret sauce of #ServantLeadership
- Look for opportunities to speak praise,
inspiration & encouragement into others.
@mwdeterding

_____

_____

_____

138

Your words & attitude affect people. Do they respect, honor, encourage & build esteem? @mwdeterding

_____

_____

_____

139

Speak life-giving words into people.
Encourage, compliment, credit
achievements, express gratitude, and offer
hope. @mwdeterding

_____

_____

_____

140

Daily best practice of #ServantLeadership:
Find one person who needs to hear
you say, "Thank you. I appreciate you."
@mwdeterding

_____

_____

_____

About the Author

Mark Deterding is the founder and principal of Triune Leadership Services, LLC. In 2011, he formed Triune Leadership Services to follow his passion of working with leaders to help them develop core servant leadership capabilities that allow them to lead at a higher level and enable them to achieve their God-given potential.

Prior to Triune Leadership Services, he worked for 35 years in the printing industry, holding senior leadership positions at Taylor Corporation, RR Donnelly, and Banta Corporation. He is an accomplished executive with a proven track record for developing purpose-driven, values-based teams that drive culture improvement, enhance employee passion, and improve business results. His work on culture transformation is highlighted in Ken Blanchard's book, *Leading at a Higher Level*, and he has been a featured speaker for the Ken Blanchard Companies Executive Forum in both 2007 and 2011. He regularly speaks to organizations and executive forums on the principles of servant leadership and how to practically apply it to their lives.

As an executive coach and consultant, he specializes in working with high-performing professionals to develop their capabilities and achieve their objectives. Working with organizations, leadership teams, and executives one on one, he helps bring focus, clarity, and action to make things work.

In addition to his duties at Triune Leadership Services, Mark also serves on the Board of Directors for the Unity Foundation in Alexandria, MN, for Mt. Carmel Ministries in Alexandria, MN, and NorthStar Christian Academy in Alexandria, MN.

He is married to his wife, Kim, and they have two sons, two lovely daughters-in-law, and two wonderful grandchildren, with a third on the way.

A m p l i f i e r™
Democratizing Thought Leadership

The Aha Amplifier™ is the only thought leadership platform with a built in marketplace making it easy to share curated content from like-minded thought leaders. There are over 25k diverse AhaMessages™ from thought leaders from around the world.

The Aha Amplifier makes it easy to create, organize, and share your own thought leadership AhaMessages in digestible, bite-sized morsels. Users are able to democratize thought leadership in their organizations by: 1) Making it easy for any advocate to share existing content with their Twitter, Facebook, LinkedIn, and Google+ networks, 2) Allowing internal experts to create their own thought leadership content, and 3) Encouraging the expert's advocates to share that content on their networks.

The experience of many authors is that they have been able to create their social media enabled AhaBooks™ of 140 AhaMessages in less than a day.

Sign up for a free account at
http://www.AhaAmplifier.com today!

Please pick up a copy of this book in the Aha Amplifier and share each AhaMessage socially at
aha.pub/servantleadership.

Go to Triuneleadershipservices.com and provide your name and email address and I'll send you the Triune Leadership Services blog each week. I will also send you a copy of my 35 Days of Encouragement Challenge. Feel free to email me at Mark@Triuneleadershipservices.com to discuss possibilities on how I can help you in your journey towards servant leadership. It just might change your life!

CPSIA information can be obtained
at www.ICGtesting.com
Printed in the USA
LVOW01s1929170317
527569LV00002B/2/P